To SHARON—
I HOPE THAT YOU
AND GREG HAVE MANY
GREAT WILDERNESS ADVENTURES
TOGETHER HERE IN ARKANSAS!

Tim J. Ernst

Kings River Falls, Kings River Natural Area

Autumn reflections, river rocks, Caney Creek Wilderness, Ouachita National Forest

ARKANSAS PORTFOLIO

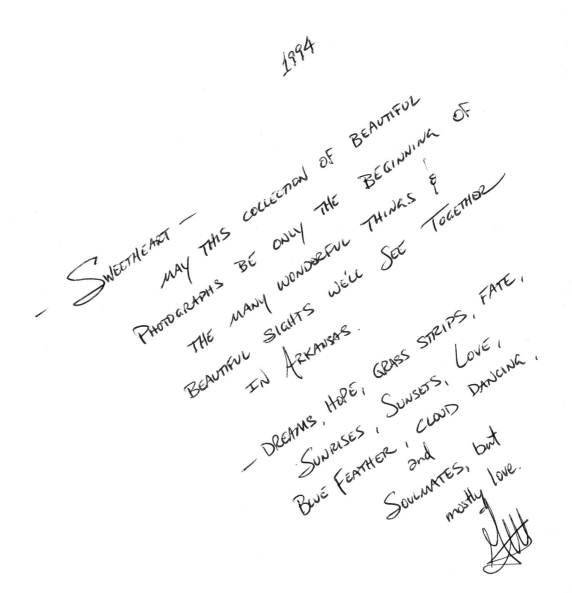

1994

Sweetheart —
May this collection of beautiful
photographs be only the beginning of
the many wonderful things &
beautiful sights we'll see together
in Arkansas.

— Dreams, hope, grass strips, fate,
sunrises, sunsets, love,
blue feather, cloud dancing,
and
soulmates, but
mostly love.

Cedar tree, south rim of Mt. Magazine, Ozark National Forest

ARKANSAS PORTFOLIO

Twenty Years of Wilderness Photography by
TIM ERNST

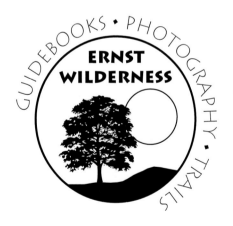

Library of Congress Catalog Card Number: 94–94452
ISBN 1–882906–14–4

Book designed by Tim Ernst
Production Manager, John Coghlan
Text editor/Jacket copy, Beth Garrett
Jacket Designer, Liz Lester

Film processed by Colliers Photo, Fayetteville
Book manufactured in Korea

Other books by Tim Ernst:
Arkansas Hiking Trails Guide
Ozark Highlands Trail Guide
Buffalo River Hiking Trails Guide
Ouachita Trail Guide
Pigeon Roost Trails Guide

All of the photographs in this book are available as
custom-printed images for your home or office wall.
The above trail guides are also available.
For current price information, or for comments and questions
about any of the photographs in this book, contact:

Tim Ernst
Ernst Wilderness
411 Patricia Lane
Fayetteville, AR 72703
501–442–2799

To mom, whose love of butterflies and flowers
taught me to relish the natural world that we live in,
and who inspired me to capture a small part of it on film.

Eastern tiger swallowtail butterfly

Sunrise from Scenic 7 National Scenic Byway, near Jasper

Contents

Star trails, north star (four-hour exposure), Pedestal Rocks Scenic Area, Ozark National Forest

Introduction

Wilderness is a state of mind. The intent of this book is to give you a tool that will put you into a wilderness state of mind as often as possible. **Arkansas Portfolio** is an attempt to illustrate the "tonic of wildness" that Thoreau said we all need.

The photographs on these pages were taken in some of the most beautiful wilderness lands in the United States. Although we don't have towering snow-capped mountains or mile-deep gorges here in Arkansas, the quality of the scenery is just as great. It is more intimate, allowing one to melt right into the landscape, instead of merely standing back and observing. You may recognize some of the scenes, since much of "The Natural State" is easily accessible. But there are many more hidden places that I wanted to show you as well.

Wilderness can be found just about anywhere, if you know where to look. It can be a vast area that one can disappear into for days, or a small moss-covered waterfall near your home. We have many 10,000 acre+ tracts of federally desig-nated and protected Wilderness Areas here in Arkansas. But we also have literally millions of acres of national forest lands, state, national and community parks, as well as private lands that are free of development.

I have devoted much of my adult life and career to not only helping to protect our wild lands, but to illustrating them as well. I have traveled and photographed all over this great country of ours, but it is Arkansas that I always return to. If you ever wonder why, just turn these pages.

This book is not intended to be a complete portrait of Arkansas—there is not enough film, nor hours in the day, available to accomplish that. It is instead intended to be a portfolio of my travels here, a record of some of what I have wit-nessed over the past twenty years. Many of the more famous spots are not included—you've seen them before, and I wanted to show you new and unique places, or present the ordinary in a different way. Some of these images may be familiar to you, though, as they have been published in numerous national, regional, and local publications of all kinds.

Many thousands of people have viewed my slide programs, and this book is an attempt to communicate the same message of wilderness in print that they have done on the big screen. In fact, this book is laid out kind of like a slide program, each photograph dissolving into the next, with a couple of pauses along the way. It is not divided into seasons, or subjects, or by geographical areas. There is no long-winded introduction—this is a *picture* book, and I know you want to get right to them instead of listening to me.

Captions with each illustration give the location and subject matter. And for those of you who are interested, there is a listing of camera, lens, and film on page 125 for each photograph as well.

The best way to view this collection of wilderness scenes is to take some time out of your busy day and view the entire book. Get a cool or soothing drink. Put on some good music (David Lanz or John Denver work well). Sit back in your favorite chair, relax, forget about the rest of the world, and travel with me into a wilderness state of mind . . .

Tim Ernst

"Going to the mountains is going home.
Wilderness is a necessity."

—John Muir

Part One

Young beech tree, bluff, Upper Buffalo Wilderness, Ozark National Forest

Polished river rocks, Cossatot River State Park Natural Area

Waterfall, hidden canyon, Richland Creek Wilderness, Ozark National Forest

Marginal wood fern, Terrapin Branch, Upper Buffalo Wilderness, Ozark National Forest

Little Missouri River, Ouachita National Forest

Under King's Bluff, Pedestal Rocks Scenic Area, Ozark National Forest

Lone mushroom, spikemoss, near Blanchard Spring, Ozark National Forest

Maple leaf, Beaver Lake State Park

Roark Bluff, Ponca Wilderness, Buffalo National River

Ox-eye daisy, along Kings River

Sunset, fall, backwater swamp, St. Francis National Forest

Hurricane Creek, sandstone boulders, Hurricane Creek Wilderness, Ozark National Forest

Lance-leaved Coreopsis, double exposure, Leatherwood Wilderness, Ozark National Forest

Sandstone formations, lichens, King's Bluff, Pedestal Rocks Scenic Area, Ozark National Forest

Richland Falls, Richland Creek Wilderness, Ozark National Forest

Sweetgum leaf and fruit, along Haw Creek, Ozark National Forest

Sumac leaf, hoar frost, Hare Mountain, Ozark National Forest

Jack Creek, along Ozark Highlands Trail, Ozark National Forest

Waterfall detail, Crooked Creek, Ouachita National Forest

Glade ferns, Indian Creek, Ponca Wilderness, Buffalo National River

Pine tree bark, needles, Seven Hollows Trail, Petit Jean State Park

Sunrise, pine trees, Forked Mountain, Flatside Wilderness, Ouachita National Forest

Limestone bluff above Shelter Cave, Blanchard Springs area, Ozark National Forest

Fire pink, phlox, Caney Creek Wilderness, Ouachita National Forest

Sandstone rocks, evening light, Richland Creek Wilderness, Ozark National Forest

Eden Falls, March snow, Lost Valley Trail, Buffalo National River

Clubmoss, pine needles, boulder, lichen, Seven Hollows Trail, Petit Jean State Park

"You must keep the land and air apart and sacred,
as a place where one can go to taste the wind
that is sweetened by the meadow flowers."

—Chief Seattle

Part Two

Spiderwort, Caney Creek Wilderness, Ouachita National Forest

Evening light, fall, Little Missouri River, Ouachita National Forest

Whitetail deer fawns, near Shores Lake, Ozark National Forest

French mulberry, along Mulberry River, Ozark National Forest

King's Bluff Falls, Pedestal Rocks Scenic Area, Ozark National Forest

46

Dogwood, October hardwood forest, Beaver Lake State Park

Mushroom family, along Lick Creek, Ozark Highlands Trail, Ozark National Forest

Liverleaf, clubmoss, Caney Creek Wilderness, Ouachita National Forest

Dew drop, leaf, Devil's Den State Park

Sunrise from Scenic 7 National Scenic Byway

Richland Creek, Richland Creek Wilderness, Ozark National Forest

Dogwood, Richland Creek Wilderness, Ozark National Forest

Cinnamon fern, Caney Creek Wilderness, Ouachita National Forest

Maple leaves, October snow, Ponca Wilderness, Buffalo National River

Post oak, sunset, Ozark National Forest

Copperhead Falls, Indian Creek, Ponca Wilderness, Buffalo National River

Mushroom reunion, Pack Rat Hollow, Ozark Highlands Trail, Ozark National Forest

Ox-eye daisy, along Cove Lake, Ozark National Forest

Maple leaf, pine needles, Devil's Canyon Special Interest Area, Ozark National Forest

Sandstone bluff, pines, Alum Cove Trail, Ozark National Forest

Sandstone shale, Cossatot River State Park Natural Area

Indian paintbrush, above Roark Bluff, Ponca Wilderness, Buffalo National River

Glory Hole, from above

Glory Hole, from below, Dismal Creek Special Interest Area, Ozark National Forest

Ox-eye daisy, along Cove Lake, Ozark National Forest

Sunrise, shortleaf pine, from Scenic 7 National Scenic Byway

Luna moth, Richland Creek Wilderness, Ozark National Forest

Inside King's Bluff, Pedestal Rocks Scenic Area, Ozark National Forest

Rock "glacier," along trail, Black Fork Mountain Wilderness, Ouachita National Forest

"Nature will bear the closest inspection.
She invites us to lay our eye level with her smallest
leaf, and take an insect's view of the plain."

—Henry David Thoreau

Part Three

Maple wings, clubmoss, near Blanchard Spring, Ozark National Forest

Maple leaves, Upper Buffalo Wilderness, Ozark National Forest

Hemmed-In Hollow Trail, March snow, Ponca Wilderness, Buffalo National River

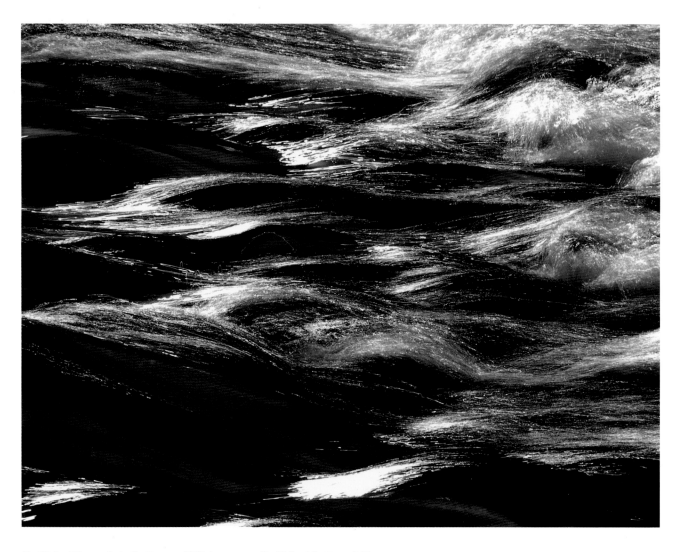

Buffalo River detail, Ponca Wilderness, Buffalo National River

Sunset from White Rock Mountain, Ozark Highlands Trail, Ozark National Forest

Beech tree leaf, club moss, Marinoni Scenic Area, Ozark National Forest

Morning fog bank, Big Piney River drainage, from Home Valley Bluff, Ozark National Forest

Northern maidenhair ferns, Upper Buffalo Wilderness, Ozark National Forest

Backwater swamp, morning light, Cadron River drainage

Young maple trees, Flatside Wilderness, Ouachita National Forest

Kings River detail, Kings River Natural Area

Pre-dawn, Lake Fayetteville

Liverwort, along Whitaker Creek, Upper Buffalo Wilderness, Ozark National Forest

Lance-leaved Coreopsis, larkspur, daisy fleabane, Arkansas River Valley

Dogwood leaf, pine needles, lichen, boulder, Flatside Wilderness, Ouachita National Forest

Hawksbill Crag (Whitaker Point), hikers, Upper Buffalo Wilderness, Ozark National Forest

Whitetail deer fawn, along Ozark Highlands Trail, Ozark National Forest

Sunrise, morning fog, Little Red River

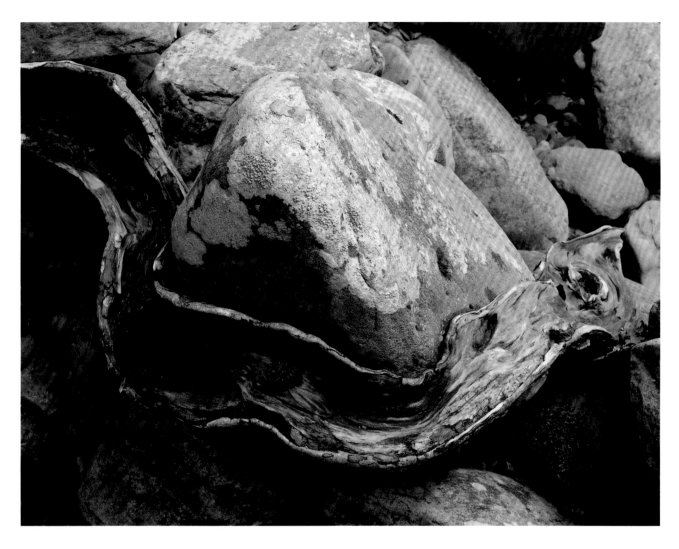

Sandstone boulder, weathered root, Hurricane Creek Wilderness, Ozark National Forest

Tunnel Cave Falls, ferns, Indian Creek, Ponca Wilderness, Buffalo National River

Hemmed-In Hollow, March snow, Ponca Wilderness, Buffalo National River

Fire pink, bluff, Caney Creek Wilderness, Ouachita National Forest

Wild azalea, Marinoni Scenic Area, Ozark Highlands Trail, Ozark National Forest

Roark Bluff, morning fog, Ponca Wilderness, Buffalo National River

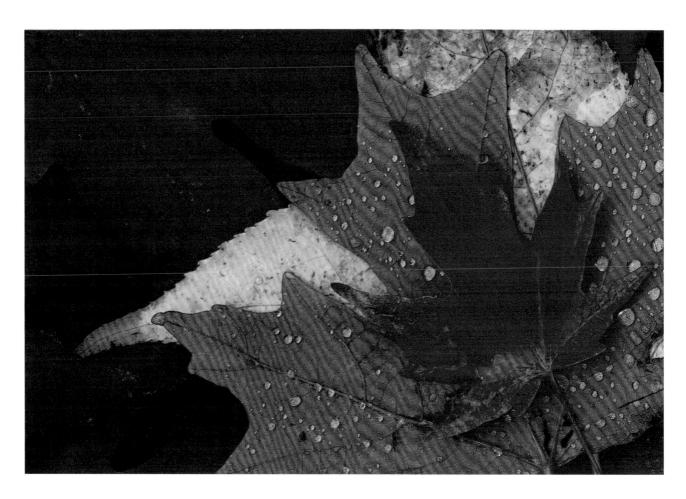

Maple leaves, October dew, Buffalo Wildlife Management Area

Hemmed-In Hollow Falls, limestone bluff, Ponca Wilderness, Buffalo National River

Yellow lady-slipper orchid, Lake Ft. Smith State Park

Willow trees, morning mist, Shores Lake, Ozark National Forest

Cossatot River, sandstone shale, Cossatot River State Park Natural Area

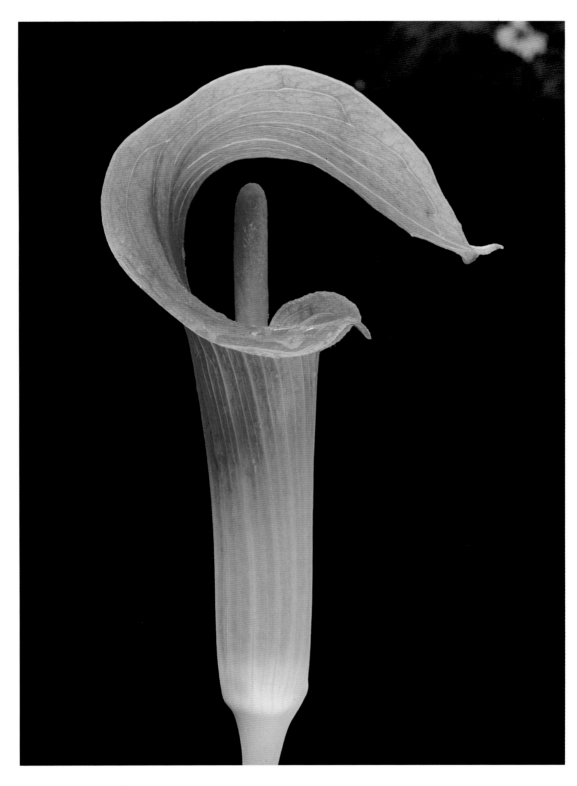

Jack-in-the-pulpit, Upper Buffalo Wilderness, Ozark National Forest

Headwater cypress swamp, Louisiana Purchase State Park

Spiderwort, sedge, Caney Creek Wilderness, Ouachita National Forest

Frog Bayou Creek, afternoon sun, Ozark National Forest

Early morning blue light, sandstone boulders, Richland Creek Wilderness, Ozark National Forest

Maple tree, near White Rock Mountain, Ozark National Forest

River rocks, sandstone shale, flood depression, Cossatot River State Park Natural Area

Waterfall #4, clubmoss, Ozark Highlands Trail, Ozark National Forest

Maple leaf, October snow, Ponca Wilderness, Buffalo National River

Upper Eden Falls, Lost Valley Trail, Buffalo National River

Indian paintbrush, cedar tree detail, Ponca Wilderness, Buffalo National River

Fall colors, White Rock Mountain, Ozark Highlands Trail, Ozark National Forest

Spiderwort, Caney Creek Wilderness, Ouachita National Forest

Hemmed-In Hollow Falls in winter, limestone bluff, Ponca Wilderness, Buffalo National River

Sunrise from Brush Heap Mountain, Athens-Big Fork Trail, Ouachita National Forest

Photography Equipment and Techniques

Here is a list of the four camera systems that I have used over the years, and the lenses that went with them: **NIKON F2/F3/FM** (35mm format), 20mm, 24mm, 28mm, 35mm, 55mm micro, 60mm micro, 105mm micro, 200mm micro, 300mm, 500mm (all lenses Nikkor); **ZONE VI** field camera (large format—4"x5"), 90mm, 120mm, 210mm, 305mm (all lenses Schneider); **LEICA R6** (35mm format), 21mm, 28mm, 60mm macro, 100mm macro, 180mm, 350mm (all lenses Leitz); and **PENTAX 6/7** (medium format), 35mm fish-eye, 45mm, 75mm, 105mm, 135mm macro, 300mm (all lenses Pentax).

I use the Pentax 6/7 system now, and absolutely love it. The gear is built like a tank, and is simple to use. It "shoots" like a 35mm, but the transparencies are nice and big. I also carry a Nikon FM with a 60mm micro lens for close-ups.

Other equipment that I carry in/on my f64 camera backpack includes a Pentax digital spot meter, OAK Photographic Society framing guide, Schneider polarizing filters, warming filters, cable releases, a collapsible light reflector, lens cleaning stuff, a tripod, and lots and lots of film (total weight over 40 pounds).

The film of choice for me in the early years was Kodak *Kodachrome*. Today, I usually shoot Fujichrome *Velvia*. The rich, saturated colors of this film make me think of Arkansas! There are a lot of great new slide films out these days—like *Lumiere* and *Provia*, which are nice too (and more to come in the future).

Film processing is critical. The first stop that I make when I return from a shooting trip is at Colliers Photo on Dickson Street here in Fayetteville. They do all of my processing, do it in a hurry, and do it right. Discount store processing may be cheap, but nothing costs more than ruined film.

My camera is always attached securely to a tripod. The Ries tripod with Bogen ball head that I use weighs nine pounds. It's wooden, bends back from the contorted positions that I often force it into, and is able to stand up to the extremely tough abuse that I give it. The legs swing up so that I can get right down on the ground with the camera. It's along on all photo excursions.

The equipment that I use is not cheap. The polarizing filter alone costs $250. The tripod, $400 (without ball head!). But the last thing that I want when that once-in-a-lifetime image presents itself to me is equipment failure. It often takes me hours, days, and perhaps even weeks to get into position to get the shot that I want, and a single failure can ruin everything. And, quite frankly, I'm not very nice to my gear. It gets tossed around a lot, and makes an unexpected scenic trip over the side of the cliff once in a while. My insurance agent doesn't like to hear from me. But, hey, cameras and lenses are the tools of my trade—I work them hard, and expect them to perform without a hitch.

Exposures for the most part were unrecorded. Few serious photographers actually record their exposures, unless they are testing film or equipment, are trying to illustrate something, or are shooting the unusual. (The exposure data that you see published in magazines is usually guessed at.) I do record long exposures, though, which are quite unpredictable.

Long exposures are what make all those waterfall pictures so neat—I just love the milky, spun-glass effect, and can't ever seem to get enough of them. There is an entire book's worth of waterfall pictures in my files. Once this spring, I shot nine different waterfalls in a single day—they were *everywhere* (only one of those appears in this book). Long exposures are also often required for shooting close-ups on overcast days. The mushroom and moss picture on page 19 was a two-minute exposure. And how about that four-hour exposure on page 10!

Some of the most frustrating time that I spend in life is waiting for the wind to stop, so that I can make a long exposure of a flower or leaf. Close-up objects must be *absolutely* still, or will not photograph crisp and clear. I like to shoot rocks—they don't sway in the breeze! It's hard to drum up much sympathy for me though—I've spent some memorable quality time waiting out the wind, or for the light to get just right. After all, I could be stuck working in a real office, only looking at pictures, instead of being part of the scene.

You hear a lot of photographers talk about the "statements" that they are making with their photographs, what they "wanted to say" with this shot or that shot. That's terrific. Wish I could do that. For me, when the film is loaded and the cameras are working, I'm on a mission. A mission that is pure and simple—I hunt for a scene that will *look good* on my wall. Period. I want to capture a little part of Arkansas wilderness, reach right out there with that lens, etch it onto my film, then reproduce it so that I will be able to enjoy it for a long time to come. And of course, I want others to be able to see that little slice of wilderness too. I want to share the beauty that I was fortunate enough to be around to witness. That's it. No secrets. No statements. You only have to push *one* button to take a picture.

As far as technique goes, I have very little. My photography is pretty straight forward—I try not to use gimmicks to alter the scene. Oh sure, I will use a sunset filter once in a while, but my intent is to render the scene the way my heart saw it, not to alter reality. I seldom "arrange" things—the patterns and compositions are already there naturally—I just have to look long enough to find them. OK, so I did include that weird shot on page 107. I really felt surrounded by all the trees in that swamp, and the fish-eye lens was the only way that I could show that. The red filter was just for fun.

If there is one thing about my work that stands out to me, it is my desire to produce a scene that is clean and free of distractions. I'll spend ten or fifteen minutes walking/crawling around with my framing guide to find the angle with the best look to it. Just moving a few inches to isolate the subject against a dark background often makes all the difference in the world. Then I study the image in the viewfinder. Is there a twig in the way, or a bright spot to ruin the scene? Anything lurking there at the edges that doesn't look right? Click. Click. I shoot a lot of film. Changing exposures. Switching lenses and angles. Film is cheap.

Light is such a terrific thing. It's what makes photography possible in the first place. The direction and quality of it makes the scene brilliant or moody. Many great photographs are taken within an hour before or after sunrise and sunset. Cloudy days are good too, and changing weather usually creates dramatic scenes. The quality of light at these times is magical. It's also pretty special during spring mornings and autumn afternoons. I swear there are times here in Arkansas when you can literally stick your camera out the window and shoot a masterpiece without trying! But consistently good photography takes a great deal of hard work (I often get up at 3am and hike several miles in the dark for a sunrise), cooperation from Mother Nature, and lots of luck. Especially luck.

There are many scenes I've known about for years, that I know will look great on film, but have been unable to record. Some places I return to again and again, hoping for all the right things to happen. A few scenes remain only in my mind, and have never been captured the way I want them. I'll keep trying.

Over 90% of my pictures end up in the trash, not quite good enough to represent Arkansas wilderness. It is only once in a great while that I am able to accurately portray how wonderful a scene really is. The pictures in this book were selected from over 100,000 images in my files, and from nearly a million slides overall. Good grief, only a million pictures? I've got a lot of work to do. I've only seen a tiny part of Arkansas, and each little corner has amazing and wonderful things to photograph. Time to head to Colliers and buy some more film!

Illustrations List

About This Book

Ansel Adams is to blame for this book. Although I never met this greatest of all landscape photographers, his work has moved and inspired me most of my life. I always wanted to make an "Ansel Adams" book of Arkansas wilderness scenes. Ever since I picked up a real camera and started taking serious pictures, this book has been my goal. It has taken me this long to put one together not because of a lack of material, but because I felt the material was not good enough. Although I will never be the photographer that Ansel was, I feel that Arkansas itself is a great enough subject to be worthy of a book. I hope that **Arkansas Portfolio** proves that to be true.

Beth Barham, an old high school sweetheart and wilderness companion of mine, was the first person outside of my family to recognize some degree of talent in my work. She beat the bushes and got my first public print exhibition at a bank in Ft. Smith in 1978. I had been working as a professional photographer for several years by then. Towards the end of 1979, I had grown tired of my commercial photography business (*Photographs Unlimited*), and sold it to my partner Phil Ezell. Phil had put up with my "wilderness" pictures long enough.

I thought that I might be ready to spring my nature photography on the unsuspecting world, but was unsure that I would be able to make a go of it. The turning point came when my dad, in our last conversation together, said that he supported my desire to make it as an outdoor photographer. He died later that day, and I knew that's what I was meant to do. Soon after, I sold a photograph of Alaska to the largest selling calendar in the world, and I was on my way.

Then I met my friend and mentor Boyd Norton, a world class photographer, writer, and defender of wild things. I was struck by the fact that he was a "real" person, not some bigger-than-life icon that I thought all photographers in his class were. He encouraged me to work in my own backyard, and his influence refined my techniques. I must have been talking about producing this book even back then (1980), since he autographed one of his books to me with "Good luck with the Ozark project." I have since enjoyed many sunsets, conservation discussions, and fine beers with Boyd, and am grateful for his gracious input.

As the years rolled on, and my files of wilderness scenes from Arkansas piled up, I began to sell more of them to national publications. Ken Smith, a fellow trail volunteer, introduced me to Matt Bradley, a great photographer, who helped get my work included in several *National Geographic* publications, which of course increased the size of my skull. Matt has since helped me out in countless other ways too, including picking the cover of this book.

I traveled to wilderness areas around the country and came back with some nice images, but preferred to spend most of my time shooting right here in Arkansas. I approached several publishers about my book idea, but none were interested. They would have been happy to produce a black and white book, but to me there is too much color in Arkansas. Ansel could have done it, but not me. So I continued shooting, improving the images, exploring more natural areas.

Along the way I became involved in the fight to establish official wilderness areas here, which included going to Washington to testify before Congress. We got some terrific areas protected, but they are not enough, and the fight goes on to secure more lands for future generations to enjoy.

Hiking trails have taken up a considerable amount of my time. Our little volunteer club (the Ozark Highlands Trail Association) has contributed over 300,000 hours of labor to trails since 1981. All of these activities contribute to my ability to be out in the woods—I often spend over 200 days a year working in the wild. It's a tough life, but someone has to do it. (Notice the grin.)

The trail projects that I've been involved in have given me the opportunity to write and publish a number of trail guides. These books have sold well throughout the United States, and have encouraged a lot of folks to visit our great state and hike our trails. I feel that if people are exposed to something beautiful, they will make an effort to protect it (and other like areas) in the future. So I have never hesitated to show someone photographs of wilderness areas, or direct them to one—they need "the tonic of wildness" as much as I do.

In 1993 I realized that it was time to finally do something with my picture book project. There were publishers interested in it at last, but their lengthy publishing schedules put the date years into the future, and I just couldn't wait any longer. So I decided, what the heck, I'll take a deep breath, sell my soul, and do it myself. And that's what I've done.

The first thing that I did was put together a great creative team to work with. John Coghlan found one of the best printers in the world to print and bind this book, and worked out all the physical details of the production. Liz Lester put up with all of my finicky demands and designed a jacket that I hope looks great in your living room. And Beth Garrett has been along every step of the way. She researched the quotes, edited text, and wrote the jacket material. It was her enthusiasm that made me decide that now was the time to do this book. I guess if it is a flop, I can blame her. Of course, I'll take all the credit if it works!

There have been lots of other folks along the way that I have not mentioned yet who have contributed in one way or another to my photography career, or to the production of this book. These include: Richard Cecil, my brother-in-law, who gave me my first camera (a Minolta SRT 100); Herb Evans and John Thomas, who worked with me at Blanchard Cave, and encouraged me to burn some film both above and below ground; Neil Compton, whose pictures from the Buffalo River showed me early on that Arkansas was indeed a very special place, and who has continued to play a role in showing me terrific areas to photograph; David Sloan and Sharon Bass, both with the University of Arkansas Department of Journalism when I took my one and only photography class (they published the first sets of my pictures, in black and white, in *Arkansas* magazine); Martha Hill, former picture editor of *Audubon* magazine, who I learned a lot from through osmosis; Dyan Zaslowsky, a great writer and friend, who has counseled and encouraged me for many years; Joe Ownbey, who got me started in my professional photography career in the first place; Greg Heinze, who knows more about my work than anyone, and has had to put up with my ravings about this book for all these years (we've consumed many bottles of gin—to go with Thoreau's tonic—while chasing after the perfect photograph); Gary Wyatt, Dan Wickliff and all the staff at Colliers Photo, where I not only buy all of my film, processing, and photo equipment, but where I always find answers to technical questions about my craft; Dr. Edwin Smith from the University of Arkansas, who helped with plant identifications; Dewey Watson and Tom Ferguson from the Ouachita National Forest, who sent me to some terrific scenic areas; Mort Gitelman for loaning me his equipment when I got desperate; Bryan Kellar, Gabrielle Bassett, Dennis Heter, Mary McCutchan, John and Barbara Benish, and Carolyn Crook, who all helped with miscellaneous tasks; and Keiko Peterson, Scott Crook, Carl Ownbey, Ken and Terry Eastin, and my mom for all of their endless advice and encouragement. That's the short list. There were others who directed me to shooting locations, researched quotes, gave advice on design, and reviewed stacks of photographs. This book is a reflection of all their efforts.

And a special thanks to *you*, for picking up this book and taking the time to see what wonderful scenery we have here in Arkansas. I hope that as you look through these pages, you are able to smell the flowers, bask in the glow of the sunset, get splashed by a waterfall, and drift into a wilderness state of mind . . .

127

Purple coneflower, double exposure, Leatherwood Wilderness, Ozark National Forest